3 1112 01332750 3

W9-BJL-679

YOUTH SERVICES   WITHDRAWN

E LEV
Levine, Deb.
Parker picks

STORY BOOK

DEC 2 9 2003

ROCKFORD PUBLIC LIBRARY
Rockford, Illinois
http://www.rpl.rockford.org

YOUTH SERVICES

Parker Picks

Parker - Age, 6 months

By **Deborah A. Levine**
Illustrated by **Pedro Martin**

SIMON & SCHUSTER BOOKS FOR YOUNG READERS

New York London Toronto Sydney Singapore

ROCKFORD PUBLIC LIBRARY

SIMON & SCHUSTER BOOKS FOR YOUNG READERS

An imprint of Simon & Schuster Children's Publishing Division

1230 Avenue of the Americas, New York, New York 10020

Text copyright © 2002 by Deborah A. Levine

Illustrations copyright © 2002 by Pedro Martin

All rights reserved, including the right of reproduction in whole or in part in any form.

SIMON & SCHUSTER BOOKS FOR YOUNG READERS is a trademark of Simon & Schuster.

Book design by Greg Stadnyk

The text of this book is set in Heatwave.

The illustrations are rendered digitally.

Printed in Hong Kong

2 4 6 8 10 9 7 5 3 1

Library of Congress Cataloging-in-Publication Data

Levine, Deborah.

Parker picks / by Deborah Levine ; illustrated by Pedro Martin.–1st ed.

p. cm.

Summary: When his finger gets stuck up his nose, Parker finds out that his nose-picking habit makes it hard for him to take part in other fun activities.

ISBN 0-689-83456-X

[1. Nose-Fiction. 2. Behavior-Fiction.] I. Martin, Pedro, 1967- ill. II. Title.

PZ7.L578325 Par 2002

E-dc21   00-063533

For Adin and his grandparents
(and proud pickers everywhere!)
–D. A. L.

To Gina, for all her love and support.
And to my dog, Mightyboy, who always let
me know when it was time to go to bed.
–P. M.

This is Parker.
Parker picks.
He's been picking a long time.
In fact, Parker's been picking
as long as he can remember,
and he's getting very good at it.

Sometimes Parker picks and flicks
it in the fishbowl.

Sometimes Parker picks and sticks it to the wall.

Sometimes he even picks
and feeds it to his dog.

Parker's finger is just the right size for picking. On a really good day, he can almost tickle his brain.

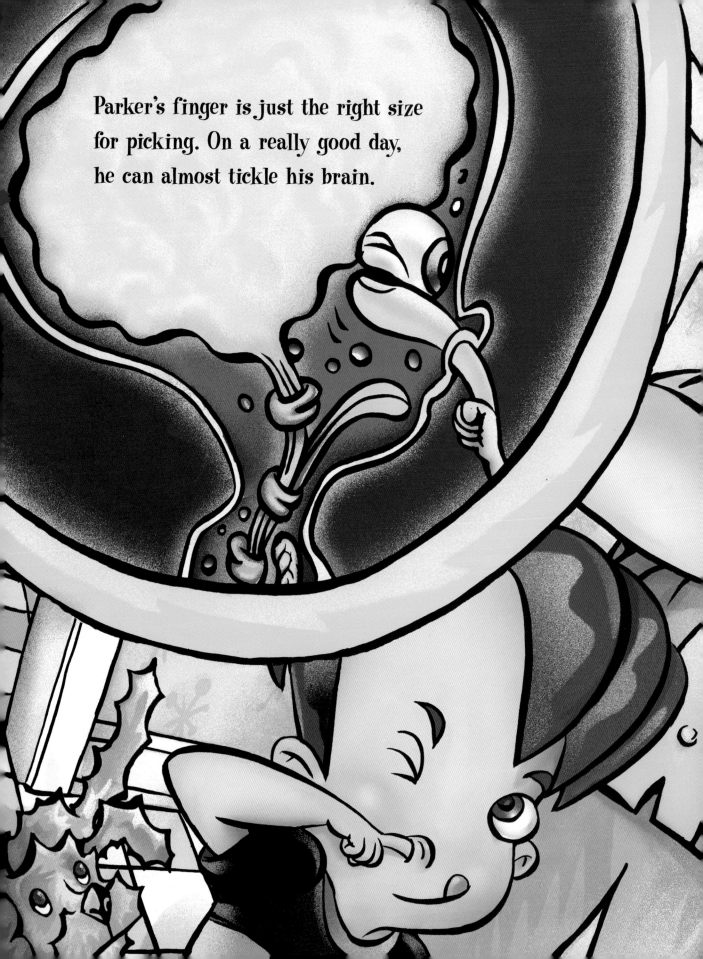

Parker's mom and dad do not approve.

His older sister thinks it's gross. (Eew!)

And his teacher does not allow it in class.

But Parker doesn't care. These opinions come from people who have never picked their own noses, and they don't know what they're missing.

One Saturday, Parker came down with a cold. His nose was stuffy and swollen, but even that didn't stop Parker from picking.

Parker was just finishing off a particularly huge pick when all of a sudden his finger wouldn't budge.

He tried and tried to pull it out.
But it was no use. The finger was stuck.
Parker was in a state of permanent pick.

Parker's parents tried everything they could think of.

Even the doctor ran out of ideas.

All anyone could do was wait and hope that eventually, when it was ready, Parker's finger would come out on its own.

The following Monday was better than Parker expected. Since he couldn't write, he was excused from taking his spelling test.

Then on Tuesday, his mom had to cancel his piano lesson.

On Wednesday, he got out of doing his chores.
Things were definitely looking up.

Until Thursday, that is, when Mr. McSweeney made him sit on the bench during dodgeball.

Friday was worse.
At Zachary Porter's
bowling party, all
    Parker could do was
    watch. And watching
    is not nearly as much
    fun as bowling.

On Saturday, Parker's dad took him to a
baseball game to cheer him up.

They had great seats, right behind first base, and Parker even caught a ball.

The crowd cheered for the little boy who had made such a great catch. They whistled and yelled when they saw the ball fly into his mitt.

But the "hoorays" turned to "hee-hees" when Parker's picture filled the screen above the field. There was Parker, in all his glory—a grin on his face and a finger up his nose.

Everybody started to laugh.

Parker started to cry.
He cried for the rest of the game . . .

and all the way home.

That night he even cried himself to sleep.

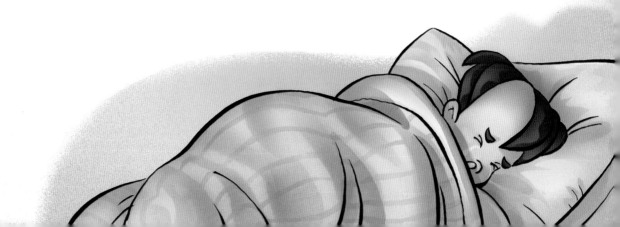

And maybe it was all that crying that finally did the trick, because the next morning, Parker woke up to discover that his finger had come unstuck.

Parker was so happy that he promised his mom, his dad, his sister, his teacher, and himself that he would never, ever pick his nose again.

And he hasn't.

Now he picks his scabs.